# Evangelicals, Obedience and Change



by

**Trevor Lloyd**
*Vicar of Holy Trinity Church, Wealdstone, Harrow, Middlesex*

**GROVE BOOKS**
**BRAMCOTE NOTTS.**

## CONTENTS

| | | Page |
|---|---|---|
| 1. | Nottingham '77 | 3 |
| 2. | 'The Evangelical Party'? | 7 |
| 3. | Worship and the Arts | 10 |
| 4. | Change | 13 |
| 5. | Congress Themes | 14 |
| | Appendix: Glossary of Congress Terminology | 22 |



ACKNOWLEDGMENTS

Quotations from the National Evangelical Anglican Congress (NEAC) Statement (which is published by C.P.A.S./Falcon under the title *The Nottingham Statement*) are printed by permission of the NEAC Executive Committee.

The quotation from *The Changing World* (ed. B. N. Kaye) on page 6 is printed by permission of Wm. Collins and Sons Ltd., the publishers of the three Congress booklets. (For details of these see the footnote on page 4).

GLOSSARY ILLUSTRATIONS

. . . are by Taffy

*First Impression* April 1977

**ISSN** 0305 3067

**ISBN** 0 905422 10 4

# 1. NOTTINGHAM '77

## Who, what and why?

2,000 delegates met at Nottingham University from Thursday 14 April to Monday 18 April 1977, in the second National Evangelical Anglican Congress. The Congress was visited and addressed by both Archbishops, attended by a number of bishops and also observers from the General Synod, the World Council of Churches, the British Council of Churches, the Roman Catholic Church, the Free Churches, the Orthodox Church—including Derek Pattinson, Secretary-General of the General Synod, Donald Wright and Colin Peterson, the Appointments Secretaries for the Archbishop and the Prime Minister respectively. The *Church Times* wrote in its editorial that the Congress 'demonstrates the vitality of the Evangelical movement. Probably no other section of the Church of England has the strength to organise such an assembly'[1]. Over 40,000 copies were sold of the three paperbacks containing the pre-congress material. These volumes contained remarkable evidence of the breadth of vision of evangelicals and their willingness to think radically while at the same time, as the *Church Times* said, 'determined to be faithful to the tradition implied in the common title of these three books: *Obeying Christ in a Changing World.*' But despite the increasing maturity and influence of evangelicals in the Church of England (nearly 50% of those being ordained now are evangelicals, for instance) the Nottingham Congress was not intended, John Stott, the Congress chairman, said, to be 'an occasion for triumphalist trumpet-blowing nor an exercise in party propaganda.'

That this intention was fulfilled is shown by the Declarations of Intent and the long Congress Statement, containing genuine expressions of repentance, humility and open-mindedness in the face of some of the big issues of our time. The new evangelicalism is by no means riding high on a 'we know it all' wave.

What, then, was the purpose of the Congress? Back in 1974, when the preparation began, various things were in mind: the need to bring the 'centre' and the 'constituency' together, to increase mutual understanding and trust, to develop a common vision of where evangelicals were going, to take stock, looking back at the Keele Congress ten years earlier, to look in depth at the theme of social ethics on which Keele had been weak, and to major on renewal, mission, and evangelism: all these things received varying emphases as the Congress planning went on. Any triumphalism belonged to Christ alone. As John Stott said in his opening address, 'We meet at Nottingham four days after Easter, celebrating the triumphant resurrection of Jesus our Lord . . . It is under the authority of Christ that we are gathered.'

The 'constituency'—the ordinary evangelical in churches up and down the country—was well represented. 41% of the delegates were lay men, 26% lay women, and 33% clergy. The high proportion of young delegates was encouraging. Raymond Turvey, Congress Treasurer, thought the number of lay people present was one of the main differences from Keele. 'We deliberately planned it over a weekend.'

[1] 15 April 1977.

And it was the delegates who were the key hard-working people. And hard-walking, too, from one side of the mile-long Nottingham campus to the other ('walking is a good congress activity' one committee member had replied to earlier suggestions of bicycles or minibuses). The structure of the Congress demanded a great deal of participation. Reading the relevant chapters in the three books, sending in responses on these to the authors (about 33% of the delegates did this), spending two-thirds of most of the main sessions in small groups of ten for discussion and amendment of the draft statement, which was changed in some cases almost beyond recognition: all this meant delegates were thoroughly involved, many able to say of the Statement, 'Yes, I got that phrase in.' Even so, the process was open to criticism. 'The Congress was solidly middle-class', wrote one observer, 'Maybe that is inevitable if you start on a Thursday afternoon and major on drafting and redrafting documents at *Times/Telegraph* level or above.' And the words of another observer, James Robertson, of USPG, were echoed by many: 'We all tasted too many themes superficially.' 'We can only skim the surface in the groups and cannot really deal with the draft statements adequately,' said Peter Cottingham of Christ Church, Barnet. John Tiller, of Christ Church, Bedford, said: 'I think the groups revealed widespread ignorance on many issues, and I think the educative role of the Congress will be as significant as the statement of our present mind, which is obviously divided, uncertain, or uninformed, in many respects.' These facts, plus the fact that the Statement was approved by sub-plenaries for which the Congress divided into nine sections, and not by the Congress as a whole, ought to be borne in mind when studying the Congress Statement.

The Statement, the Congress chairman announced on Saturday morning, was not intended to be a comprehensive statement of evangelical belief, but to help delegates do a serious and responsible job in clarifying their thinking, and to help communicate the thinking of the Congress to those in the churches. But it was limited in its agenda to the three Congress books.[1] This announcement succeeded in removing some of the frustration from delegates who had been attempting detailed amendments of the draft statement, and encouraged them to grapple with the big issues before the Congress.

But it does raise the question of how the particular issues in the books were chosen. For instance, Christian teachers were up in arms about the content of the chapter on 'Education and the Law', saying it should have been written by a teacher rather than by David Harte, lecturer in law at Newcastle University. But what many did not understand until the Congress began was that the main subject under discussion was the law, with education simply being an example of the outworking of this.

Similarly two other chapters gave rise to revolts during the Congress sessions. In the session on 'The Power of the Media', Raymond Johnston and Michael Saward of St. Matthew's, Fulham, who interviewed him, majored on the 'power' part of the title, as did the chapter in the book. Some

[1] *Obeying Christ in a Changing World:* Vol. 1, *The Lord Christ* (ed. John Stott); Vol. 2, *The People of God* (ed. Ian Cundy); Vol. 3, *The Changing World* (ed. Bruce Kaye) Fount Books (Collins), February 1977.

thought this approach 'negative, intemperate, unfair to those in the media, not recognizing the good things', as author Os Guinness expressed it. So he and actor Nigel Goodwin led a group of seventy or so, including radio and television producers and writers, out of the session to produce a more positive statement under the chairmanship of Sir Norman Anderson, chairman of the General Synod's House of Laity. Many people again were confused by the title of the session on 'The Gospel and Culture', which had nothing whatever to do with the arts, and concentrated almost entirely on race relations, naturally chosen by David Bronnert, who works in Southall, as the example to highlight the problems of cultural alienation. But there was applause for the man who said, 'We have an absence of *rapport* with British working class people,' and a group was set up to draft a statement on the deprived inner-city areas. It is some evidence of the open way in which the Congress was conducted that the results of these two 'rival' statements can be found in the final Statement.

But what was the process by which subjects were originally selected ? The Congress Planning Committee decided not to invite a number of authors to write papers for the Congress, but to set up research groups to select 'the major burning issues which in their opinion *must* be included in the Congress agenda.' Over 150 theologians and 'experts' were involved in six groups. To help them they had three things. First, a very wide-ranging list of topics, both to stimulate them and to define the area in which they were working. For instance, a group on 'Personal Discipleship' had: 'Christian initiation and baptism with the Spirit, experience and theology, maturity as human beings (emotional and spiritual, different kinds of counselling), the occult, personal ethics and lifestyle, work, leisure and wealth, evangelical spirituality.' To look again at such lists is to be forcefully reminded both how much the Congress needed to narrow the range of subjects to be tackled (even if some were confused or felt the wrong subject had been given priority) and also how much work has still to be done by evangelicals in fields they have hitherto ignored.

The second thing the groups had to help them was the general theme of the Congress—the renewal of the church in a changing world, as it was at that time. This meant that each group had to take serious account of changes in modern society, and to relate the subjects chosen both to this and to the theme of church renewal.

The third item of help came in the form of a paper from the theology group on 'Method in Theology'. Part of this is reproduced at the beginning of the introduction by Bruce Kaye to the third of the Congress paperbacks, *The Changing World,* and the approach to it is thoroughly presented in Tony Thiselton's paper in the first volume, on 'Understanding God's Word Today.' 'The development,' says the *Church Times* editorial, 'is simply the recognition that there are great modern problems which should not be dismissed in advance by a drawing up of the bedclothes to shelter the converted individual or by the incantation of selected Scriptural texts.' Or, in the less colourful words of the paper itself, 'though we shall certainly be given some light, enough to live by in obedience in the present, we cannot guarantee that either in our preparatory research or in the Congress itself we shall be given answers that are either simple or final.' Because this was an important factor in the way the preparatory work was done, and thus affected the final Statement, it might help to quote Bruce Kaye:

> 'Traditionally, Evangelicals have done their theology by trying to work out the basic principles from the Scriptures and then by either applying these principles to the question under discussion or seeking to discover their practical implications. We might call this a deductive approach to doing theology. The method which has been adopted . . . runs in the opposite direction, without, however, denying the propriety of the older method. Here an issue in the present situation has been taken, and then analysed in depth to see what is at stake in it and how Christian truth can be related to it. We might call this an inductive approach to doing theology.'[1]

It is a bit like doing two bits of mapwork and then exposing one to the other to see how they relate: the mapwork of the contemporary human situation, studied in depth with an awareness of one's own presuppositions and reactions ('Why do I see the problem as having that shape rather than another?'), and the mapwork of each Bible passage, its context and the situation to which it was written, again with an awareness of one's own presuppositions and traditional ways of interpretation ('But I always thought it meant . . .').

So the topics were selected, the groups reshaped, the eighteen paper-writers chosen by the groups, who then continued to help, stimulate and correct the thinking going on in each subject. So the papers were written, published and read. And in the light of the responses received to the papers, each author drafted his section of the statement and prepared in a half-hour interview to respond to the responses. During the Congress, one day was devoted to each of the three books: *The Lord Christ* on Friday, *The Changing World* on Saturday and *The People of God* on Sunday. Each day began with a presentation in dramatic form of the theme for the day, followed by two sessions (one before, one after, lunch) in which the paper-writers were interviewed by an appointed interviewer for half an hour: they were often questioned from the floor, and then the draft statement was discussed for an hour. This meant that each person attending the Congress had to choose two out of the six papers in each book, and attend those sessions. During the afternoon there were also practical workshops on a wide variety of optional subjects: Audio-visuals, drama, television, inner city housing, local radio, etc., including a large two-day workshop on evangelism. Then in the evening there was some worship, a preacher on each of the four evenings, a dance presentation from St. George's, Leeds on Friday evening ('You have to pay to see them dance like that in the West End,' said one bishop), a sound-slide presentation by John Gladwin from Durham and John Forrest from Thames Television on Saturday, and the Communion Service on Sunday evening. After this there were comeback sessions with the authors from 9.15 to 10.30 p.m. for any who wished to continue the discussions begun earlier in the day. Finally, the statements were re-drafted in committee in the light of the day's discussion of each topic, and this process continued into the small hours.

[1] *The Changing World* (Collins, 1977), p.9.

## 2. 'THE EVANGELICAL PARTY'?

One significant question hanging over the start of the Congress was whether there was still a definable evangelical party, or whether the Congress would reveal such divisions as to make it apparent that evangelicals could no longer act together. John King had asked in an article in the *Church of England Newspaper* at the beginning of the month, 'the delegates . . . will have to decide which they want: an Evangelical unity which is preserved by tucking inconvenient questions under the mattress or a unity of *some* evangelicals behind an agreed policy which bears some relation to the days in which we live.' John Stott, asked at the opening press conference what tensions he thought would arise, said, 'It won't be the charismatic movement: I guess that the publication of *Gospel and Spirit*[1] has defused the issue before the Congress.' That this was true seemed apparent both in the dicussion of those parts of the statement that touched on this issue (A.9, G.2, H.7, L.5) and also in the atmosphere of love ,joy and understanding which was apparent especially on the occasions when both large groups and small groups met for worship. Another possible cause of tension was whether the Congress could agree to say anything about the revision of the Series 3 Communion Service, in the light of the fact that Roger Beckwith, Warden of Latimer House, Oxford, had already published his desire for revision in three areas: eucharistic sacrifice, prayer for the departed, and reservation. Again, though there was opportunity for discussion of this, it came to little and in the Statement (F.3 (d) and (e)) the Congress welcomed many features of the service while expressing concern both about the areas mentioned and about the fact that a number of evangelicals were seriously disturbed by them.

Far from marking either the beginning of a new 'party' discipline or the end of evangelical coherence within the Church of England, the Congress seemed determined to show clear adherence to evangelical essentials while allowing for the widest possible expression of belief on other matters. 'One of the main reasons why some sections are longer than others,' says the introduction to the Statement, 'is that they include a diversity of viewpoints.' The Statement Steering Committee, meeting for several hours from 10.30 each night in the comfortable dungeons below Cavendish Hall, was not spending its time squashing minority opinions or deciding on a party line. 'The reason we've been up so many hours,' said John Stott, 'is because of our desire for integrity, so that the Statement accurately represents what was discussed.' Hence the immediately apparent muddle and duplications in the Statement, and the not infrequent use of 'some of us think . . . and some think . . .' (representing a 50-50 division of opinion) and of 'we believe . . . but also a substantial majority say . . .' (representing a 60-40 division). Each part of the Statement

1 Published in April 1977 by both the Fountain Trust and *The Churchman* (in its April issue), this joint statement by a group nominated by the Church of England Evangelical Council and the Fountain Trust reveals a wide area of agreement and understanding on matters that have been thought to divide. Only four of its seventeen signatories were not involved in planning for or speaking at the Nottingham Congress.

attempts accurately to represent what those who actually discussed it thought—which is why apparent contradictions occur (e.g. compare F.1(d) with J.2 and 4). One of the most significant things about the Congress was not the Statement it produced, but the 'Nottingham spirit' of openness to one another, willing to disagree openly, yet united in sharing a common obedience to Christ. And John Stott reminded the delegates on the opening evening that the main purpose of the Congress 'is not to produce a Statement, but to meet each other and above all to meet the Lord Christ, to let him stretch our minds, to celebrate his supreme Lordship together.' 'As an observer,' said Brigadier Fred Hoyle of the Salvation Army, 'NEAC was a heart-warming and mind-stretching experience. One of the most forceful impressions received was the sincerity of the delegates in their desire to know and to be involved in the Lord's will.' And this feeling was echoed by many. 'If it's a party, I'm not in it,' said one high-ranking evangelical. 'I don't like to think of evangelicalism as a party,' said Sir Norman Anderson in his closing address, 'but as a tradition with certain fundamental convictions.'

So the call from the *Church of England Newspaper* (among others) for clear, unequivocal statements on matters such as the ordination of women, support for the Programme to Combat Racism, patronage, etc. went unheeded. To have produced resolutions on such subjects would have meant voting them through, perhaps by only small majorities. Instead, what was said in the Statement perhaps more accurately reflected the general feeling of evangelicals as represented at Nottingham.

But it does leave us the question, 'What are the fundamental convictions which unite evangelicals?'—or, as one reporter asked at a press conference, 'What is an evangelical?' John King headlined this the next morning in the well-produced but controversial *Church of England Newspaper* daily bulletin: 'Hundreds of delegates would go home happier if they knew the answer without having it wrapped up in incomprehensible jargonese. The question of identity should be at the top of the list at NEAC. How can we know where we are going if we do not know who we are? What is an evangelical?' But he had to wait until the end of the Congress for an answer from chairman John Stott, who said in his closing address: 'I am aware that some of you are suggesting we drop the epithet (evangelical) and it is time we merged in the main stream of church life. Certainly we shouldn't retain the word because we are cussed or obstinate, or to make us feel comfortable or more secure, or because we live in the past. We retain the designation because we have convictions: We evangelicals are Bible people . . . and we evangelicals are Gospel people.'

This clear note at the end of the Congress was a help to many, not least those non-Anglican evangelicals who were there, who had to some extent been estranged by the total commitment to the Church of England which was the outcome of the Keele Congress (L3 and the fourth Nottingham Declaration of Intent spoke of 'insensitivity' and 'grief' at this and pledged closer fellowship and co-operation with them, though one Baptist present rightly pointed out the difficulty of reconciling this declaration with Declaration 7 committing evangelicals to seek 'the unity he wills' with Roman Catholics—despite the fact that this is to be 'in obedience to our common Lord and on the basis of Scripture'). Michael Hews of Scripture Union, a non-Anglican, said, 'Particularly heartening to Free Church evangelicals was John Stott's reaffirmation in his closing talk that Anglican evangelicals are "Bible people" and "Gospel people".' In speaking clearly of the need to be biblical ('We deplore the cavalier and sometimes arrogant attitudes to Scripture which are flaunted in the Church today . . . We see it as part of our responsibility to remind our own church of its stance . . .'), John Stott stressed the need to be 'more conscientious in our study of the word (. . . the word surely that will always be associated with Nottingham is this blessed word hermeneutics[1]) and more radical in our application.' 'If Scripture is supreme over traditions, that includes both our Anglican traditions and our evangelical traditions . . . Nothing is sacrosanct to the radical conservative evangelical Christian except Scripture itself.' This highlights two significant developments among evangelicals over the last ten years, which were much in evidence both in the preparatory material and at the Congress itself: the growth of a more mature method of biblical interpretation and theological method, and the comparative[2] freedom from past slogans in the radical application of Scripture to life today.

John Stott's second point—'We evangelicals are Gospel people'—highlighted the centrality of the Gospel as he spoke of the good news of freedom ('from guilt to forgiveness'), the good news of a new society ('The Gospel we have preached in the past has been too individualistic. The Church is part of the Gospel') and the good news of a new world. 'A Gospel which makes us want to sing and dance and leap for joy, as William Tyndale said. Who wants an irreducible minimum Gospel? . . . Let's celebrate it with uninhibited joy in our worship.'

1 For an explanation, see below, p.15.

2 I say 'comparative' because, though this freedom was apparent in most of the 'platform and many of the delegates, there was a tendency in the amending of the draft statement to vote for the re-insertion of the recognizable 'slogan' words, perhaps because some felt lost without them, perhaps because many felt they might draw delegates (and those especially back home in the larger suburban traditional evangelical churches which were very well represented at the Congress) together under a familiar banner. For instance the first sentence in D.1 was not there in the original draft, which was more directly concerned with interpreting and understanding the Bible than with its nature.

## 3. WORSHIP AND THE ARTS

### Worship

And sing and dance and leap for joy they did. There was the sheer thrill of singing with 2,000 other people, to music provided by Noel Tredinnick and the All Souls' orchestra. 'Jesus is Lord, creation's voice proclaims it' appeared to be the favourite hymn! Indeed, despite the inclusion of 72 hymns in the Congress booklet only 20 were used, almost exclusively familiar ones, none from the 'Changing World' section and hardly any of the new material being prepared for a new hymn book in the language of the *Good News Bible.* Perhaps this unadventurousness simply reflects normal parish churches! The lack of thoughtful, reflective hymns, the almost total absence of silence, the small amount of time given to God-centred reverence and awe were, one hopes, not typical of our parish churches. (But see Declaration of Intent 12 admitting 'low standards in our worship.') 'So seldom were we open to the numinous,' said one Anglo-Catholic observer.

However, despite the criticisms, there was a helpful blend of large group (2,000 together each evening) and small group (10 or so meeting for a short time before breakfast each morning)—advocated in F.1 (a) and (b). Openness and love were more easily demonstrated in the fellowship of the latter, but even in the 2,000 on Sunday morning and evening the times of prayer in groups of six ('If your chair is unhooked, turn it round and start praying with those behind you . . .') really took off because of the immediate sense of unity and purpose in these groups. The Sunday evening Communion, at which the Archbishop of Canterbury preached and Michael Baughen presided (assisted by a random collection of 42 delegates and observers, including one nun and one American lady presbyter, for the smooth-running administration) 'was immensely impressive in its blend of informality and dignity,' said Gordon Ogilvie of St. James', New Barnet. 'It alone pointed the lesson that the informal need not be banal or sloppy.'

It was good that much of Sunday morning's presentation was given over to worship because, as Colin Buchanan pointed out, the theme had very little treatment in the preparatory Congress books. So delegates enjoyed an exceedingly humorous and pointed sketch from the St. John's College, Nottingham informal dance drama group, in which a very solidly minuet-dancing black-coated congregation underwent a revolutionary change in their worship by considering how they behaved during the rest of the week. If churches put this into practice it would mean encouraging different styles of music in worship, dancing, ministering to each other (this involves talking in church!), using the gifts of the congregation—even if the 'gift' is the ability to play a drum solo, and much more openness to the expectation that God might communicate in ways other than the sermon.

In the Statement itself there is a whole section on worship (F.3). One sentence clearly reflects the Congress worship (F.3(c)): 'We commend experimentation with drama, dance, music, movement, colour, furnishings and setting to heighten the awareness and involvement of God's people in true worship.' The opportunity for joy, flexibility and involvement in worship in Series 3 is welcomed, while at the same time some serious statements are made about deficiencies in the Series 3 Communion Service. One of these (F.3(e)) uses the technical word *anamnesis.* Many argued against using such a technical word because of the difficulty of explaining it to people in the parishes, but as David Gregg (a staff member of the Board of Mission and Unity)[1] pointed out, it was doubtful whether a sub-plenary session could in five minutes provide a simple answer which had eluded the church for several centuries of debate. The word remained, a plea for the reinsertion of a full stop between the celebrating and proclaiming of Christ's death at the end of paragraph 29 and the celebration of the other events in the life of Christ.

One of the other concerns of the Congress about worship was the need to reflect the local culture, 'In a belief that in a multi-cultural area churches should be multi-cultural and varied' in worship (F.2(b); T.4)

**Creative Arts**

One of the most obvious things at the Congress was the impact in both worship and presentations sessions of drama and dance as means of communication. The Breadrock team, led by Murray Watts (who with Paul Burbridge also led an afternoon workshop on drama) won immediate *rapport* with their audience as they pursued what the *Church of England Newspaper* rightly saw as a medieval pattern: 'Knock-about shepherds wondered what their wives would have to say to them when they got home late reporting a vision of angels; a red-nosed clown built his house on sand; Zacchaeus . . . showed a touch of demagoguery that in its way out-Heroded Herod.' 'I enjoyed Breadrock most', said Harry Sutton, Canon Missioner of the South American Missionary Society, 'I found it wholly stimulating and exciting—not just the meticulous care to detail, but it was God-honouring in ability and technique.' 'It demonstrated effectively that there are other ways of communicating truth than sermons which are as meaningful in their own right,' said Scripture Union's John Tigwell.

Not everyone was that happy, and some expressed doubts about the use of drama in worship as a means of involving people emotionally, or about the portrayal of Christ, or the use of humour—sometimes the Breadrock humour was pretty savage, and Murray Watts admitted the Monty Python influence on his generation but defended the 'sudden death' theme in their drama because it is so serious you have to laugh at it: 'It *is* something we fear in modern society.' To those who said that while some of the drama was very moving, some was trivial, he answered that drama is like that (fair enough!) and explained that in their usual medium of street theatre they needed to build up from the crowd-attracting trivial to the more serious. 'Is this sort of thing worth doing badly?' one delegate asked, conscious of

[1] He is the author of a scholarly monograph discussing this point: *Anamnesis in the Eucharist* (Grove Books, Liturgical Study No. 5, 1976).

the group's professionalism. 'Yes' was the short answer, provided that those involved really wanted to communicate better and were prepared to learn. 'The main thing about much Christian drama is not badness but wetness—cringe factor,' said Murray Watts. But despite the doubts, the drama made people talk and was clearly welcomed by the delegates, if the applause was anything to go by.

This sort of reaction heralds a new evangelical openness to the use of the body and of creative arts in both worship and communication: a sort of rejoicing in creation which has been lacking in a group traditionally dominated by more 'Puritan' thinking. This found expression in the revolt in the section of the Congress discussing the media, where a group led by those involved in the arts turned their backs on discussing power and control and effect in relation to the media, and gave themselves to producing a statement (P.3) which is very positive in tone. This calls attention (P.3 (a)) to our immense heritage of cultural riches in Western Europe and says, 'Evangelicals can rejoice in this rich legacy and can also play their full part in its continuing creative development at all cultural levels in the media.' As it affects local churches rather than those professionals involved in the arts, it should mean churches giving consideration to how to encourage and develop the artistic abilities of their members, how to support financially those seeking involvement in the 'foreign cultures' of the mass media, how to contribute to local radio, how to educate Christians about the media so that criticism can be informed. The whole section on the media ends (P.5) with applause for those who have 'heeded the Keele challenge to enter a career of whole-hearted professionalism in the work of the mass-media. May that process continue and accelerate to the glory of God.'

## 4. CHANGE

Obviously, with suggestions such as those in the previous two sections being envisaged, together with calls for the restructuring of the church, for the 'visible unity of all professing Christians' including the Roman Catholics (M.3 (a)), and for the total involvement of Christians in politics, the media and the concerns of the third world, the idea of change was on the delegates' minds. Stuart Blanch, Archbishop of York, caused a few shudders (and much laughter) when he said in his opening address, 'The 1662 service has for me now the charm of total unfamiliarity.' Calling for 'a new generation of militants within the church . . . a new generation of thinkers, willing to get behind the ways in which we usually express ourselves . . . a new generation of contemplatives . . . a new generation of prophets with a vision of society under the sovereignty of God', he ended with a sentence quoted again by a number of delegates, 'We can expect and welcome change as the angel of the changeless God.'

Given such a challenge, and a Congress theme that originally majored on the theme of renewal, it is a little surprising that there is little directly about the subject of change in the Statement. Perhaps we need more work to be done on the pastoral, psychological and sociological problems of change both in society and the church, and the problems that arise when a dogmatic application of the theology of the church comes up against the various expressions of English folk religion which give a certain amount of stability and security to our society.

F.2(d) calls for sensitivity, dialogue, love and time for adjustment for those in changing situations. This spirit was well illustrated in the Congress itself. One delegate thought significant 'the insecurity of a number of older delegates particularly clergymen: this demonstrates the need for effective and continuous dialogue amongst evangelicals'. There needs to be a determined effort to put this into practice, for instance at Diocesan Evangelical Unions.

But while all this is true, there is in the Statement a curious mixture of all-embracing, God-centred radicalism and a clear 'non-budge' stance on some of the practical issues which non-evangelicals might find a little curious, but which are none the less genuinely held convictions. For instance, there is the urgent radicalism of A.6: 'We commit ourselves to pray, teach and work until the whole church is so transformed by God's Word and Spirit, that it offers the authentic and attractive Christian alternative to life without Christ.' And there is a no- (or little-) budge position on theological colleges (J.5, K.5); on patronage (K.6); and on the Protestant nature of the Establishment (K.7), despite the efforts of one bishop to get delegates to include the Roman Catholic Church among the other churches the Congress decided should be asked to share 'the ancient constitutional ties that establish her as the church of this realm.' No doubt there will be 'ongoing discussion' as the Statement often says, on these issues . . .

## 5. CONGRESS THEMES

### Jesus and Salvation

It is to another area of change and no-change that we turn next. There is always bound to be tensions among evangelicals—as among all Christians—between those who are attempting to re-state the Gospel and Christian doctrine in modern terms and those who see the Gospel, stated in the previous generation's thought-forms, as something to be defended at all costs. Perhaps one of the significant things about the Congress was that it revealed that this debate is in fact going on among evangelicals, a debate which would hardly have been possible even ten years ago. So it was that Michael Sadgrove and Tom Wright (who made a name for himself at the World Council of Churches Assembly at Nairobi in 1975), 'the youngest faces among the pundits,' (as the *Church of England Newspaper* said) 'said things which were surprisingly conservative, but looked like a sell-out to some.' 'The Gospel is made up of a "whole salvation story" from Abraham onwards. Cries went up that the Cross was being undervalued, but this was the panic caused when traditional words are not used.' The struggle can be seen for instance in C.1 (a): 'It is the whole work of Jesus Christ that brings salvation, which is anticipated in the Old Testament, unfolded in his ministry, completed in his death and resurrection . . . We give various emphasis to the various biblical expressions of Atonement. Some see the truth that Christ died in our place as the central explanation of the cross, while others, who also give this truth a position of great importance, lay greater stress on the relative significance of the other biblical pictures.' Here, one suspects under the pressure to achieve agreement on the text of a statement, the language used is less than precise. But the significant thing is that here is honesty and openness in debate: how easy it would have been simply to have carried the day on the old slogans! And the next two paragraphs are rich in their exploration of the Christ-centredness of salvation, while firmly stating: 'In the New Testament Jesus Christ is unequivocally the only Saviour.'

The section of the Statement just before this one (B: Jesus Christ the Lord) though more precise in its wording, also shows evidence of commitment to the debate on Christology (the doctrine about Jesus Christ) and ends, 'We urge evangelical scholars to play their part in the current discussions on Christology. But the incarnation and atonement have to be acknowledged as mysteries greater than man's mind can completely grasp.'

The background to this discussion during the Congress was the showing over Easter of the Grade/Zefferilli epic 'Jesus of Nazareth' on ITV, followed during the Congress by the BBC 2 enquiry presided over by Don Cupitt, 'Who was Jesus?' This latter gave rise to a resolution passed virtually unanimously on the last day of the Congress calling on the Archbishops 'publicly to confirm that the Church of England still stands by its historic faith in the Christ of the Scriptures and the Creeds.' But the debate will continue, with evangelicals arguing in perhaps a more informed way against the current dominant humanitarian Christology. Declaration of Intent 1 is a commitment to just that.

## Understanding the Bible today

'I heard of one delegate who thought that Hermann Neutics was a German professor of theology', said David Watson as he began his address on Friday night; but by the end of the Congress there can have been few delegates unaware of the importance of the way we interpret and understand the Bible today. Tony Thiselton (demonstrating his learned absent-mindedness by hunting for an overhead projector slide until a delegate called out 'Is that it in your hand?'—it was!) originally intended his paper to cover simply the use of the Bible. But now the Statement includes a sentence on the nature of Scripture (D.1) and a paragraph (D.5) on the authority of Scripture. The central thing coming across to the delegates, however, was neither of these issues, but the need for immense hard work (to which delegates are committed in Declaration of Intent 2) in both a thorough examination of the context, or 'horizon' of the writer[1] and a proper assessment of the assumptions brought to the text by the reader or his 'horizon'. 'If getting at the original meaning of the Bible is such hard work,' asked John Goldingay in his interview, 'what about the young Christian who's not yet had time?' Tony Thiselton's answer was perhaps another blow at protestant 'private interpretation', but clearly part of the new realism evangelicals have about the church. If the young Christian is going to base a decision for his future on this verse of scripture then he must go to the Christian community: not just his own Bible Study group, but the wider Christian fellowship, Scripture Union notes, etc. These features come across in D.3 and D.4: 'The fellowship of the Christian Church makes possible a wholeness of understanding that transcends what is possible to individual hearers.' The danger of 'instant application', of forcing the Bible to answer distinctively modern questions to which the text does not refer, is also underlined.

## The Church

Here the theme of renewal comes to the fore, with complementary calls to restructure the church and to change the life-style of the church, and the Declaration (12): 'we pledge ourselves by prayer and action to seek renewal in our local churches.'

The call for restructuring (E.6, F.1 (a) and (b), H.5) majors on the need for small groups, so that the church will grow in both maturity and numbers. It is interesting to work out the agenda for such groups, many of the delegates (and this is another difference from Keele) having considerable experience in churches which have small groups. There are words of warning: E.6 (a) expresses sadness because independent house churches are not linked to the 'historic Christian community' (i.e. the local church), and F.1 (b) speaks of the need for the small group to have a direct link with the major congregation—and patterns right and wrong for this were discussed diagrammatically in the interview on this subject. Para-church structures and the voluntary principle (see Glossary and K.4, E.4, E.6 (e)) got a mention but little thorough discussion apart from the knock sponsored by student chaplains in favour of 'integrating people into the local worshipping community.'

1 This whole issue is dealt with in a clear and very readable way in the pre-Congress paperback *The Lord Christ,* on pp.99-113, with a number of examples which lend themselves to discussion.

If there are thriving, warm-hearted, Christ-centred, mission-oriented small groups springing up at the lower part of a church structure which includes some much larger regular meeting for celebration and praise, then this itself will considerably affect the life-style of the church. In this area the statement speaks of the church embodying the gospel in its community life (A.6, E.2, expanded in F.2) and throws out various ideas for living as a 'family in community'. This included a more thorough use of Sunday, though some delegates had doubts on this because of hindering the natural family from being together, and because of the problems of Christians in non-Christian families, or on shift work. Delegates were also divided as to whether it was right to re-affirm the clear Keele commitment to the centrality of the eucharist as the main Sunday service. Many wanted guidelines for 'a simple life-style which demonstrates a joyful sharing of material and spiritual resources,' (V.9) and under the heading 'A Servant Church' called for the relinquishing 'of historic but pretentious titles, over-elaboration in ceremonial and dress . . .' 'Some of us have scraped it off our labels with a razor blade,' said the Venerable Timothy Dudley-Smith. Yet Michael Baughen was still able to call Dr. Coggan 'Your Grace'.

**Initiation and Membership**

This subject is dealt with at a number of different places in the Statement, reflecting both a different angle (whether you see it from the point of view of Christian beginnings generally, or as belonging to the Church as an institution, whether you see it from the angle of the doctrine of the church or from the viewpoint of those in the local church taking on-the-spot decisions about pastoral policies) and also an obvious difference of opinion among the delegates. A sizeable number of delegates wanted to vote (G.3) for the abolition of infant baptism. The original draft of G.3 acknowledged the validity of infant baptism 'with the proviso that the response of faith is an integral part of sacramental initiation . . .', the final statement calls here for 'the necessity for a personal response of faith' to be 'made clear in any future amendment to the form of service.' This seems possibly at variance with E.3: 'The church on earth is marked out by baptism, which is complete sacramental initation into Christ and his body', which could be interpreted in an entirely different way, unless the idea of the response of faith has been imported into the word 'baptism'.

The natural evangelical tendency towards making possibly subjective demands is taken further in K.3 where applicants for membership of the electoral roll would have to 'make some current declaration of Christian faith, and some recognition of financial responsibilities.' (Perhaps the last bit is pretty objective, though . . .).

Comparing the statements in F.3 (f) and G.3, G.4 with the Keele Statement, to which G.3 refers back, there is a simple loss of clarity because of having two statements on the subject, but not that extreme weakening of the Keele position which some delegates feared after the first day's session on 'Christian Beginning'. Indiscriminate infant baptism (i.e. the baptism of children whose parents are not obviously practising and professing Christians) is still a scandal, and there is a renewed call for a baptism policy. The very words of Keele are used about baptisms taking place at public services of the church. But the Statement is aware of the Ely report (which it urges the Church to reconsider) and of the Synod debate on initiation. As at Keele, there is a division between those who wish to see children of Christian parents admitted to Communion and those who do not, with F.3 (f) (i) and (ii) much stronger on this than G.4. What is very apparent is that this debate cuts across the old churchmanship divisions, and that the keenness of the theological arguments in favour of child communion is felt most by the increasing number of evangelicals in churches which have a parish communion as the main service. As numbers of candidates for adult baptism increase, so the anomaly of having confirmation following it has emerged more strongly than at Keele. The phrase 'baptism . . . is complete sacramental initiation' (F.3 (f), cf E.3) entails the abolition of confirmation in such cases, just as it leads to the call for child communion following infant baptism.

**Gospel, Mission and Evangelism**

This theme, though prominent in much of the original thinking of the Congress Planning Committee, does not appear very prominently in any of the three preparatory paperbacks, though it was intended that each paper should be written in the light of it. But, partly because of the effect of putting together 2,000 people concerned in various ways with both mission and evangelism and partly because of the action of pressure groups like that composed of secretaries of missionary societies demanding a fuller statement on the priority of preaching the Gospel to be inserted before the statement on Global Stewardship, action was taken to ensure that the theme figured in the Statement . . . . For those not familiar with the very clear definitions of GS 222, paragraphs A.3 and A.4 should help people distinguish between mission and evangelism. 'Both evangelism and social action are, therefore, universal obligations laid upon us by the authority of Christ,' says the Statement, losing none of the Lausanne commitment.

Some people had hoped that the Congress would come down decisively in favour of the 'let my people grow' project[1], or of the wider discussions following on from the Archbishops' 'Call to the Nation' and pointing to some kind of national mission or celebration of the faith. To be fair, the Congress did not major on this sort of issue, but it is significant that the two sentences in the Statement on this are in a low key. Expressing gratefulness for the Archbishops' initiative, A.4 goes on: 'and still hope that some kind of "Mission to the Nation" may follow it. At the same time, we are concerned that regional enterprise is greatly preferable to a centrally imposed plan.' Especially significant is the high place given to the local church in evangelism, both in this section ('we . . . commit ourselves to the task of evangelism, especially through our local churches') and in others (A.6, E.6 (b), F.1 (e), G.1, U.1).

Global mission is rightly seen as extending to this country (U.1: 'We welcome the increasing recognition by the church in this country that it is in

1 This was the title of a duplicated report by an Evangelical Alliance working party on evangelism in 1976, and it is not to be confused with a book by Michael Harper of the same title (Hodder, 1977)!

a missionary situation'). A worldwide sharing in mission, ministry and suffering is envisaged (U.2, U.3). This is rather oddly put in H.3 where 'the suffering of our brethren' got changed to 'the suffering of people throughout the world', making our desire 'to share . . . their suffering, that we may share their maturity' sound potentially very different from the desire to learn from the maturity through suffering of the church in Africa. Present at the Congress were two Ugandan bishops Festo Kivengere and Misaeri Kauma, who had been out of the country following the death of the Archbishop, Janani Luwum. Bishop Kivengere was given a very warm welcome when he spoke movingly on the Saturday evening of the Archbishop's death being like the grain of wheat dying. The Congress passed a resolution expressing shock, asking for action from the U.N. and O.A.U. 'to bring Uganda back to the rule of law', and asking that the Government should not allow President Amin to attend the Commonwealth Conference. And the destination of the £4,600 collection at the Communion service reflected this global vision: it was divided between the Janani Luwum memorial fund, TEAR Fund, the EFAC Bursary Scheme, the Evangelical Anglican Missionary Societies and the Archbishops Council on Evangelism.

## Ministry

The main assertion here is that (J.1) 'Christianity is a one-caste religion', and this clear abolition of the clergy-laity distinction in ministry led even to the cutting out of the phrase 'both clergy and laity' from Declaration of Intent 5, which pledges delegates to seek ways of making every-member ministry 'more effective in all our churches'. E.3 (c), F.3 (c) and H.6 all call for the implementation of every-member ministry, while K.2 by implication can envisage the Church of England ideal of resident, geographically-based ministry being one which is plural, non-ordained and unpaid (or possibly 'lay'?). The pattern envisaged in J.2, J.3, J.4 is the creation of a local, ordained group of presbyters 'who *may* include women and will absorb and replace Readers.' That this is not the only pattern under discussion by evangelicals is shown by the inclusion in F.1 (d) of a call for lay presidency at the eucharist. Both in F.1 (b) and J.2, J.4 there is a tacit assumption of the priority of the existence of the church over against the existence of a full-time paid ministry, with the call not to amalgamate parishes simply because of the shortage or cost of full-time clergy. It would be good to see this worked out in the continuing discussions on the implementation of the Sheffield Report.

Another of the main emphases, a corollary both of every-member ministry and of the concept of a shared, plural, local leadership in the church (J.2, J.3, F.1 (c),) is on the need for training at every level, from children (G.4) to the whole congregation (A.10: 'a comprehensive and flexible programme of lay Christian education which should be adapted to people of differing ages, cultural backgrounds and educational abilities.' F.3 (c), Declaration 10). F.1 (c), F.1 (g), J.3, J.4 call for special training for different sorts of church leaders, with the emphasis taken off the academic in both selection and training.

Two predictable issues sparked off amazingly little controversy. Bishops are valued, but 'we consider the current Anglican practice of episcopacy ought to be reformed'—a call spelt out in E.6 (d), where, as in K.8, there is a desire to make the pastoral job possible, without 'excessive administrative burdens'. Women, as the *Church of England Newspaper* noted, were not much in evidence either on the platform or pushing for ordination. J.6 begins by repenting of failure to give women their rightful place, but ends with 'ultimate responsibility' (the phrase began as 'headship', changed to 'presidency' and certainly means more than bishops) 'normally singular and male.' As the *Rev.* Carol Anderson from New York said, 'the role of women in the life of the church has got to be more thoroughly discussed. There is a need to break down the roles *and* to think more carefully about the wording of documents . . .' R.7 certainly does not reveal, in its 'no change' statement, much agonizing over the problem.

**Culture**

The mixture of cultures in our society was welcomed by David Bronnert as he spoke from his experience in Southall on the subject of race relations (S.1: 'We long for a church that is enriched in its life by the varieties of cultures and races'), and those in the working group on the inner city obviously shared an enthusiasm for their area, but all this seemed to contrast with the lack of identification shown by many delegates with the problem areas' in society, coming as many of them did from the 'white highlands' of suburbia. While speaking out against the unfair discrimination of the 1968 Immigration Act and the position of the *Daily Telegraph,* David Bronnert is no militant 'Programme to Combat Racism' man, and this firm yet quieter apprach is reflected in a non-militant statement which is still warm in its call to Christians to be concerned and in its statement on 'black-led churches' (S.3, S.5, L.4). The great desire here, however, is for 'churches . . . which are culturally, racially, and socially mixed,' and for whole-hearted Christian involvement in such areas (S.6). Though it may, one hopes, have some effect on suburban churches, this section of the Statement really needs studying, defending and amending with a militant black Christian at your elbow, to be realistic. And the Congress was notable for the absence of black faces . . .

Nor were there many, apart from the professionals, involved in the culture of the inner city. Section T (amplified by N.7 (Unemployment) and echoed in F.1 (f)) laments the failure of the church in these areas and rightly sees the problem is not just in terms of communication (as at Keele) but in terms of the incarnation of the Gospel. There is evidence here of the need for evangelicals as a whole (and not just those already working in such areas) to be committed to the theological and sociological re-thinking that has to be done, for a greater degree of identification with working-class culture than was evident in the Congress.

**Involvement**

Involvement and identification were two of the key words at Nottingham as evangelicals discussed openly in public their disagreements on areas of life on which many were speaking for the first time: politics, the media, the inner city, the third world, law, education, etc. 'We see the need for a costly identification with people in their alienation' (A.4). Michael Hews of Scripture Union commented, 'Healthily, most of the Congress boiling-points were nothing to do with the internal machinery of the Church of

England. Particularly significant were the passionate concerns shown by many delegates for Jesus to be "made real to inner-city man" and for more positive Christian involvement in the arts and the media.' The possible areas of involvement seem so vast that a Church Council could well spend time considering them all and putting them in some order of priority (and then not have time to do anything about it . . .) There were calls for churches to get involved in the life of the local community (F.2 (a)), in local radio (P.3 (c)), in neighbourhood law centres (Q.1 (d)), in local politics (N.7: 'The local church has a responsibility to be alert to local events and changes as part of their care for the community', 'Apathy in politics is unchristian'). N.2 lists local and national politics, trade unions, housing associations, tenants' associations, health committees and local pressure groups as some of the areas requiring Christian involvement, 'as a vital part of the Christian vocation'. Political education is a field in which the church ought to be at work.

Perhaps particularly significant again was the openness of the split on politics among evangelicals. All seem agreed on the need for involvement, but a sizeable number could not agree with John Gladwin's moderately left-wing definition of the way in which that involvement should be spelt out, and so there is a complete alternative statement in this section (N.8), originating from a group headed by Brian Griffiths and Michael Alison, saying things like: 'We believe that the responsible ownership of private property is a Biblical mandate for a fallen world. . . . the widespread distribution of private property rights is a necessary condition in a fallen world for the development of a responsible and relatively free society.'

There were calls for Christian involvement in education (Q.2 (b) and (c), Q.3 (d) and (e)), and in the global issues of our time defined in V.10: 'the population problem, arms trading, conservation, pollution, the uncertainties of nuclear technology, unemployment, malnutrition, the persecution of minorities, terrorism . . .' Perhaps by 1987 evangelicals will have worked out more of the 'how' of all this involvement. Incidentally there is a global view of money both here (V.7) and in the section on the institutional church (K.11: 'we urge the prior claims . . . of the third world, overseas mission . . .') and both sections commend tithing. 'Ever-growing economic prosperity' is challenged in N.3 (though the creation of wealth is encouraged in the rival N.8 (4)) while in V.4 the Government is asked to set a date for the implementation of the United Nations target for official overseas aid of 0·7% of the Gross National Product ('GNP' in a Statement remarkably free of jargon initials).

**The Family**

This section of the Statement is quietly predictable (R), but reflects a great deal both of loving care and of hard thinking by evangelicals on some of the ethical issues since Keele. Thus there is 'a full welcoming place in the Christian fellowship for the Christian homosexual' (R.3), an admission that Christians are divided over 'the validity of divorce and remarriage in extreme circumstances' (a curious phrase), and a call for sex education to be placed within the context of marriage and the family. An interesting exercise would be to underline all the places where the Statement is at variance with the commonly-held view of the family in our society today. Perhaps significantly, the family is little mentioned elsewhere in the Statement (Q.2 (g), F.3 (c), M.2 (h)).

## Unity and The Roman Catholic Church

These sections of the Statement (L and M) are fairly self-contained, welcoming the unifying influence of the charismatic movement, the Ten Propositions (so long as they do not involve an ambiguous Service of Reconciliation), and the progress in doctrinal discussions with the Roman Catholic Church. It is the warmth rather than the clear demands made in these statements which is significant as a move in evangelical thinking, especially towards the Roman Catholics. Indeed there is a contrast here with a long history of hostility towards the Church of Rome, and suspiciousness has not finally died yet. There are still good reasons why evangelicals are *not* Roman Catholics. But since Keele the effects of the working out of Vatican II have made a tremendous difference. The Anglican/Roman Catholic agreements have not been (and were not at Nottingham) received uncritically, but the participation with integrity of Julian Charley—and his own commendation of the agreements—have inspired confidence.

## Conclusion

2,000 people gone home. £55,000 spent (plus another £5,300 the delegates spent on the bookstall and £900 at the soft-drinks stands). That, and four days gladly given to God. What impression had they left? 'An impression of the great vitality of the evangelical movement evidenced in enthusiasm for debate on many issues and subsequent action, in moving from initial confusion, even ignorance, and tension in early discussions to a warm, charitable consensus in subplenaries and final session, in harmony between charismatics and non-charismatics, in joyful worship,' said Canon Colin Craston, joint vice-chairman of the Congress and a member of the General Synod's Standing Committee.

Two bright magpies flew off as I walked towards them across the grass of the Nottingham campus. The attempt to get everything down in black and white, defined and agreed, has flown out of the evangelical camp. To quote Colin Craston again: 'The significance of the Congress was in the beginning of a debate on such issues as hermeneutics, Christology in late 20th century categories, the shape of the church, evangelicals and society, etc.' In other words, there is very much work still to be done, and a solemn commitment, embodied in the Statement and the Declarations of Intent, to do it. Or as John Stott summed up, 'The Nottingham Statement will come to be regarded not only as a statement of the past but as an agenda for the future. We must continue this delightful dialogue with one another.'

## APPENDIX 1: A NOTTINGHAM GLOSSARY

Despite the attempts of authors, delegates and the bleary-eyed Statement Steering Committee, the first two-thirds particularly of the Statement has many phrases and ideas in need of a Jargonese dictionary. If in doubt (or wanting to abbreviate the Statement somewhat), try the following test: put a line through any phrases in the paragraph under discussion which do not mean anything to you and then ask, what should we *do* as a result of what is left? Then move to the next paragraph, etc. Here we offer some slight help to those submerged by words . . .

Canon B.27

**'Establishment'** (K.7): Old-fashioned word for 'shop'. Used in the Church of England for the closed shop which gives exclusive rights to the C of E 'as by law established' as the state-recognized form of religion, having certain legal sanctions for its decrees and certain involvement of the state in running the church and vice-versa (eg bishops in the Lords, but appointed by the Prime Minister).

**'Canon B.27'** (G.4): not a numbered church dignitary, but one of the legal 'canons' of the church on the subject of confirmation, which the resolution of the General Synod mentioned in G.4 asserts gives bishops discretion to admit younger children. An examination of the Canon reveals the clause 'laying his hands upon children and other persons' which is somewhat qualified by the instruction to the parish priest to present to the bishop 'none but such as have come to years of discretion . . . and can render an account of their faith . . .' The bishop's 'discretion' about the age is hard to detect in the Canon.

recognizing gifts

**'Gifts'** (J.3, F.3 (c)): need to be 'recognized' and then 'exercised'. Such phrases appear in the statement to refer both to natural abilities ('He has a natural gift for playing the drums/administration/talking . . .') and to gifts which sometimes appear to by-pass the user's natural abilities (such as tongues, interpretation, healing).

ecumenical map

**'Ecumenical map'** (I.7) a well-known term invented by the author of this section for something which does not exist, namely a division of England into ecclesiastical districts, common to all denominations (see *The People of God*, p.135).

**'Hidden curriculum'** (Q.3): As opposed to 'Core curriculum' (which refers to the basic 'core' of subjects taught in a school rather than the juicy extras), 'hidden curriculum' refers to the way in which the structure and policy of both Government and Local Education Authorities in itself has a teaching content which may outweigh, for instance, any direct teaching about the value of individual human personality.

**'Indigenous'** (F.1 (c)): 'of the natives'—i.e., truly local.

every member ministry

**'Ministries'** (A.3/J.2 etc.): To be distinguished from both Government departments and the more specialized '*The* ministry' which sometimes refers to full-time(?), ordained(?), life-long(?) ministers in the church. This word is now used in the context of everyone and every church group having some particular ministry. One aspect of this is 'Every-member ministry' (H.6, F.3 (c)).

pastoral expositor

**'Pastoral Expositor'** (D.4): Usually a single minister explaining the Bible to his flock, with love and care.

**'Patronage trusts'** (K.6): Every parish has a patron, who has a right to put anyone in as the vicar of the church he is patron of. The patron may be the local squire, the bishop, a Diocesan Board, or a Patronage Trust—a group of trustees who exercise the right to nominate the new vicar.

**'Presbyter'** (J.2): Greek word for elder, used to mean someone who is ordained, but avoiding the words 'priest' or 'minister'.

ongoing discussion

**'Ongoing discussion'** (A.10): Used to be called 'dialogue in depth'. Means interminable talking, usually on subject of intense disagreement.

stipendiary 'pennies from heaven'

**'Stipendiary presbyter'** (J.2): one of the above, paid in a different way from ordinary mortals (his wage is called a 'stipend').

non-stipendiary

**'Non-stipendiary presbyter'** (J.2): one of the above, but not paid. Used to be called 'Auxiliary Pastoral Minister' but that made him sound a bit second class, like an engine on a sailing ship.

under-used plant

**'Under-used plant'** (K.10): Both rural and machine-minded interpretations of this have to be discarded in favour of 'buildings', or the resources in bricks, mortar and contents which the church has at its disposal . . .

voluntary principle

**'Voluntary principle'** (K.4 and see also V.5, 6): the principle by which societies for overseas and home mission, theological training and the meeting of human need have been established without a formal link with the church (and many of them on an inter-denominational basis) by the voluntary giving of time, money and energy by individual Christians. Congratulations to the drafter of E.6 (e) on avoiding the prevalent phrase 'para-church structures', which describes roughly the same thing.